SUPERSCIENCE

FLOWERING PLANTS

Rob Colson

W
FRANKLIN WATTS
LONDON · SYDNEY

First published in 2010 by
Franklin Watts
338 Euston Road
London NW1 3BH

Franklin Watts Australia
Level 17/207 Kent Street
Sydney NSW 2000

Produced for Franklin Watts by
Tall Tree Ltd

Editor: Jon Richards
Designer: Jonathan Vipond
Photographer: Ed Simkins
Consultant: Dr Astrid Wingler

A CIP catalogue record for this book is available
from the British Library.

Dewey Classification 582.1'3

ISBN 978 0 7496 9523 1

Printed in China

Franklin Watts is a division of Hachette Children's
Books, an Hachette UK company.

www.hachette.co.uk

Picture credits:
Front cover: main image La_torre/Dreamstime.
com, tr Gemsbok/Dreamstime.com, tc Vladimir
Ivanov/Dreamstime.com, tr Saeid Shahin Kiya/
Dreamstime.com, 1 Luis Tejo/Dreamstime.com, 3
Voyagerix/Dreamstime.com, 4 Matthias Weinrich/
Dreamstime.com, 5t Ivan Korolev/Dreamstime.
com, 5b David Coleman/Dreamstime.com, 6
redmal/istockphoto.com, 7t Attila Puskás/
Dreamstime.com, 7b Summersea/Dreamstime.
com, 8l Tyoron2 8r Pierdelune/Dreamstime.com, 9
Darren Green/Dreamstime.com, 10 Mr Poortom/
GNU, 11t Marsina/Dreamstime.com, 11b
Gemsbok/Dreamstime.com, 12 Carolina K. Smith
M.d./Dreamstime.com, 13l Yuetao Huang /
Dreamstime.com, 14 Sarah Crow/Dreamstime.
com, 16 Luis Tejo/Dreamstime.com, 17t Marbo/
Dreamstime.com, 17b Elena Ray/Dreamstime.com,
18 Saeid Shahin Kiya/Dreamstime.com, 19t Kts/
Dreamstime.com, 19b Lothar Grünz, 20l Dixi/
Dreamstime.com, 21t Robert H. Mohlenbrock, 21b
Dartmouth Electron Microscope Facility,
Dartmouth College, 22 Custom Life Science
Images/Alamy, 23t Voyagerix/Dreamstime.com,
23b Anette Linnea Rasmussen/Dreamstime.com,
24 Ken Cole/Dreamstime.com, 25t Andrey
Medvedev/Dreamstime.com, 25b Suttisukmek/
Dreamstime.com, 26 Richard Griffin/Dreamstime.
com, 27t Philip Dickson/Dreamstime.com, 27b
Eug, 28 Chewhow Lim/Dreamstime.com, 29t
Spicelines, 29b Marcin Winnicki/Dreamstime.com

*Contents

What are flowering plants? 4

The parts of a plant 6

Trees 8

Roots 10

Stems 12

Leaves and photosynthesis 14

Parts of the flower 16

Animal pollination 18

Wind and water dispersers........... 20

Seeds 22

Fruit and nuts 24

Germination............................. 26

How we use flowering plants 28

Glossary and resources 30

Index 32

*What are flowering plants?

Flowering plants are the most common types of plant on Earth. There are more than 200,000 different species of flowering plant, and they are found all over the planet.

▌Making seeds

Flowering plants come in all shapes and sizes, from a mighty oak tree 20 metres tall to the tiny watermeal, with flowers just 1 millimetre wide. They are found in fields and forests, on windswept mountain slopes and in the hottest deserts. Some flowering plants even live in the oceans. All of them produce flowers, which contain female eggs, called ovules, and male sperm, contained in tiny grains of pollen. The ovules and sperm combine to make a seed, which becomes the next generation of the plant. The seeds are often contained in a fruit.

Many different types of flowering plants grow in wild meadows, including white and yellow daisies.

▌Pollination

Plants need to send the pollen they produce to other plants. This process is called pollination. Some use visiting animals to carry the pollen. These plants often make colourful and sweet-smelling flowers to attract the animals. Other flowering plants use the wind. The flowers on these plants, such as grasses (below), are much less colourful.

Ferns such as these, which reproduce using spores rather than seeds, are known as 'living fossils' because they have been growing almost unchanged on Earth for hundreds of millions of years.

Early plants

Plants first appeared on Earth about 450 million years ago. Instead of making seeds, early plants reproduced by releasing spores into the air or water, just like the microscopic algae from which they evolved. Flowering plants that reproduce by making seeds appeared about 200 million years later. While spores can only be carried in the air or water, pollen and seeds can be carried in many different ways, including by animals. By using animals in their reproduction, flowering plants have been able to diversify, or branch out, into many more different forms than their spore-making ancestors.

*The parts of a plant

Like us, plants are made from different parts, each of which performs a particular task in the plant's life.

Growing from roots

Flowering plants may vary in shape and size, but they all have the same basic parts. Most flowering plants grow in the earth. The roots hold the plant in the ground, and also absorb water and nutrients from the soil. The stem grows from the roots and supports the plant above ground. The stem holds the flowers, leaves and fruit and carries water and nutrients to them from the roots. The leaves make sugars using energy from the Sun. The flowers are made from special stems and leaves, and are used for reproduction.

flower

leaf

stem

A sunflower is an annual flowering plant, which means that it lives for just one year.

roots

The giant lily's huge, flat leaves help it to float on the water.

Growing in water

Some flowering plants have adapted to living in water. They are known as aquatic plants and live on or near the surface of the water. Many aquatic plants are not held in place by their roots. Instead, the plants float on the water, using special sacs filled with air to keep them afloat, just as we might use arm bands to help us swim. Sea grass is a special kind of flowering grass that grows on the seabed of shallow oceans in vast underwater meadows.

Project Cells

The basic unit of life, or building block, in both plants and animals is the cell. Each cell contains a nucleus, which is the cell's control centre. The nucleus is surrounded by jelly-like cytoplasm. Within the cytoplasm are organelles, which perform different functions, like organs in our bodies. At the centre of every plant cell is a fluid-filled space called a vacuole. The vacuole helps to maintain the shape of the cell. Make a slide with a thin layer of red onion skin on it: lay the onion onto a slide with a drop of water on it and place a cover slip on top. Place the slide under a microscope at a medium magnification, and take a look at the onion's cells.

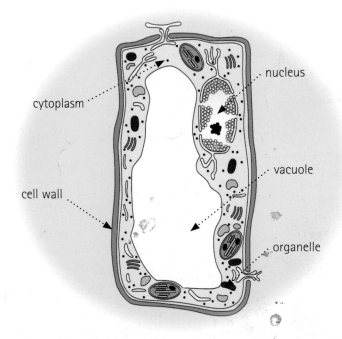

cytoplasm

nucleus

vacuole

cell wall

organelle

Plant cells all have the same basic parts. Can you see the vacuole in your onion cell?

*Trees

Trees are large plants with strong woody stems called trunks. Trees can grow more than 100 metres tall and some live for thousands of years. Some trees are flowering plants, while others are a type of plant called a gymnosperm.

Many trees grow tiny flowers every spring called blossom. Cherry trees such as this one in Japan produce spectacular white flowers.

Woody plants

Full-grown trees are generally at least 5 metres tall. Smaller woody plants are called shrubs. Branches grow off the main tree trunk, and smaller twigs grow off the branches. The branches and twigs allow the tree to spread out sideways so that all of its leaves can receive sunlight. Trees provide a home for many different plants and animals, and humans have used their wood to build and make fires for thousands of years.

Gymnosperms

Gymnosperms are plants that do not make flowers or fruit. They produce seeds on the outside of cones. Many of these seeds fall close to the plant and die, but they are hardy and may lie on the ground for a long time until conditions are right for them to grow. Gymnosperms have been on Earth for nearly 400 million years. Conifer trees are the most common gymnosperms.

The largest plant on Earth, the giant sequoia tree, which grows in North America, is a gymnosperm.

Deciduous trees

Where it is always warm and wet, as in the Amazon rainforest, trees keep their leaves all year. These are called evergreen trees. In places with cold winters or dry seasons, many trees only have leaves part of the year. These are called deciduous trees. Trees lose water into the air through their leaves, and must replace it with water taken in by the roots. When it is cold or dry, the roots cannot take in much water, so deciduous trees drop their leaves. The trees barely grow while they have no leaves. This annual change in growth makes the rings in a tree trunk – each ring represents one year of growth.

Every autumn, the leaves of deciduous trees in cooler parts of the world turn orange and fall to the ground. For a few weeks each year, they are a spectacular sight. The leaves grow back in spring.

The roots of trees can spread out over large areas. They keep the soil in place and stop it from being washed away by the rain or rivers.

*Roots

Plants take in nutrients and water through their roots. Some plants store nutrients in specially adapted roots. Roots often hold a plant securely in the ground.

Food in the soil

Most flowering plants have roots that grow into the soil, spreading out underground. This secures the plant in place. It also gives the roots a larger surface area over which to take in nutrients and water. Soil is made from tiny pieces of rock mixed in with the remains of dead animals and plants, called organic matter. The roots take in nutrients from both the rock and organic matter. Some flowering plants do not put down their roots in soil. For example, plants with aerial roots attach themselves to other plants and take in water from the air.

Root vegetables

Plants that store carbohydrates such as sugars and starch in their roots are an important source of food for humans and other animals. Carrots store sugars in the main central root, known as the taproot. The carrot plant is biennial, which means that it lives for two years. In the first year, it grows leaves and builds up the store of sugars in its taproot. It will use the energy in the root to make flowers in its second year of life, as long as we do not dig it up and eat it first!

The carrot is a root vegetable. It has been developed by humans from a wild plant to give it a sweeter taste.

The leaves of a Venus flytrap have tiny hairs on them. When an insect or spider comes into contact with the hairs, the leaves snap shut and the animal is trapped.

Carnivorous plants

In areas with poor soil, such as bogs, roots cannot absorb many nutrients. Some plants have developed clever ways to find the nutrients that they need. They catch insects! The plants set traps for the insects, and then 'eat' the trapped animal by dissolving it in digestive juices, just as we digest our food in our stomachs. Pitcher plants grow large, cup-shaped leaves to form pits into which the insects fall. The Venus flytrap has leaves that act like jaws, snapping shut on any unfortunate insect that lands on them.

*Stems

The stem holds a plant upright and supports its leaves and flowers. Nutrients and water pass through the stem between the roots and the leaves.

The work of stems

A stem is made from a series of nodes connected by internodes. At nodes, buds grow into new stems, leaves or flowers. The special kind of stem that forms the stalk of a leaf is called a petiole. Plants also store nutrients in their stems. Some stems swell to store extra nutrients for the next year's growth. Many of these swollen stems grow underground and look like part of the roots. Stem tubers such as potatoes are storage stems. Bulbs such as onions are stems surrounded by modified leaves. The rhubarb plant stores sugars in fleshy petioles.

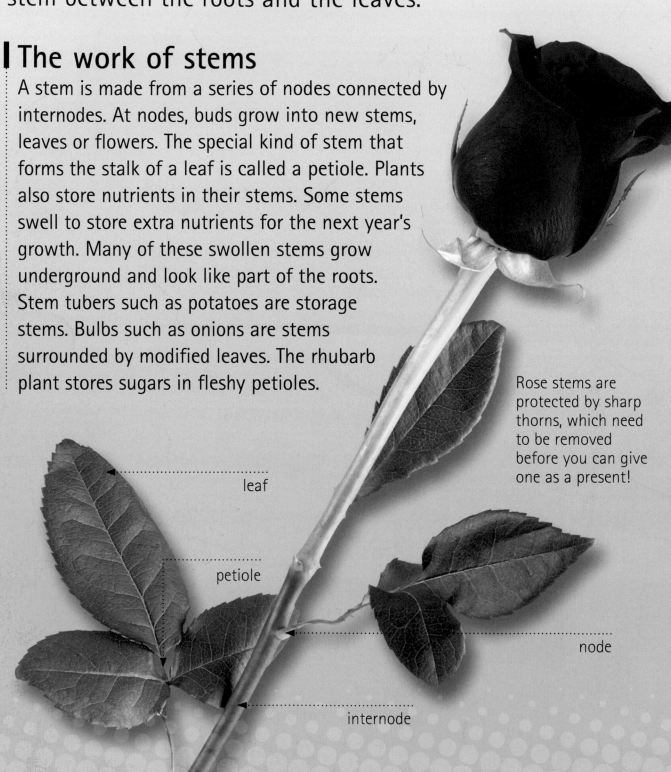

Rose stems are protected by sharp thorns, which need to be removed before you can give one as a present!

leaf

petiole

node

internode

12

Project Sweet or salty?

For this experiment, you will need six identical flowers and three vases. Pour about half a litre (two glasses) of water into each vase. Add a tablespoon of sugar to one vase and a tablespoon of salt to another. Label each vase sugar, salt and water. Place two flowers in each vase. Place the vases next to each other on a window sill and check them every day. You will discover that the flowers in the sugary water live the longest.

When you check on your vases, you will notice that the flowers in salty water (right) die much more quickly than the flowers in sugary or plain water. Salt water kills most plants. Plants that do live in salt water are specially adapted to survive in it.

Xylem and phloem

Stems contain special cells, called xylem and phloem, for transporting water and nutrients. The xylem carries water and minerals from the roots to the rest of the plant in a liquid called sap. Water evaporates into the atmosphere from the surface of the leaves, and this pulls the sap up the stem. The phloem carries sugars made in the leaves down to the roots and other parts of the plant that need them. The sap in the phloem can move both up and down a stem. In a tree, the wood is the xylem and the phloem is in the bark.

The milky sap of the rubber plant is collected and used to make rubber goods such as tyres and Wellington boots.

*Leaves and photosynthesis

Plants are crucial to all life on Earth. All our energy first came from the Sun. Plants capture this energy in their leaves in a process called photosynthesis.

Chlorophyll

Plants absorb light through their leaves using a chemical called chlorophyll. Sunlight contains all the colours of the rainbow, and chlorophyll absorbs all the colours except green, which it reflects out. This is why plants are green in colour. In a process called photosynthesis, plants use the energy from light to combine water with the gas carbon dioxide to make the sugars they need to grow. This energy can be used by humans by burning or eating plant material.

The dense rainforests contain a huge number of plants and trees, all capturing energy from the Sun.

The oxygen we breathe

As well as capturing the power of the Sun, plants are vital to the air that we breathe. When life first began on Earth, there was very little oxygen in the air, but a great deal of carbon dioxide. Plants absorb carbon dioxide and release oxygen, and over hundreds of millions of years, the amount of oxygen in the air increased. This oxygen has made animal life possible, as we breathe in oxygen and breathe out carbon dioxide. When forests are cut down, this vital balance is destroyed.

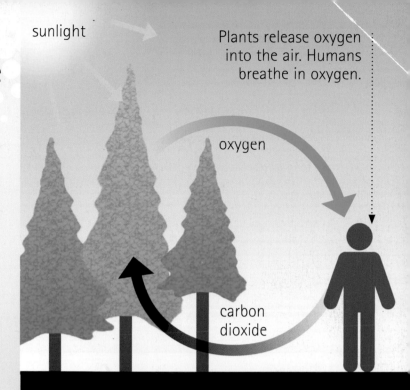

sunlight

Plants release oxygen into the air. Humans breathe in oxygen.

oxygen

carbon dioxide

The carbon cycle maintains the balance of carbon dioxide in the air. Animals breathe out carbon dioxide. It is then absorbed by plants, which release oxygen in turn.

Project What makes leaves green?

Leaves need sunlight to make energy. Without it, they will eventually die. To see this, take a healthy plant with several green leaves. Cut out two pieces of kitchen foil large enough to cover a leaf completely. Cover two of the leaves completely with the foil and secure it gently in place with paperclips. Water the plant and leave it in a sunny place for a week. When you return, take the foil off the two leaves. They will have gone a much paler green as they start to die and lose their chlorophyll. Now leave the plant for another week and see how the colour returns to the leaves now that they have sunlight again.

The covered leaves can no longer capture energy from the Sun, and begin to die.

*Parts of the flower

Plants use flowers to reproduce. Flowers are often very pretty or sweet-smelling. This is to attract animals, which carry the flower's pollen to other flowers.

The female ovules

Flowering plants have both male and female parts, although they may be in separate flowers. The carpel is the female part. The female ovules are in the ovary at the bottom of the carpel. The sticky stigma at the top catches the pollen, which travels down into the ovary to fertilise the ovules.

Petals are special leaves that are often brightly coloured to attract animals.

The **stigma** catches the pollen from the body of visiting insects.

The **stamen** makes the pollen, which contains the male sperm.

The **ovary** at the bottom of the flower contains the female ovules.

Sepals are special leaves that protect the flower while it is still a bud.

A passion flower, a plant that is visited by large bees.

Pollination

Plants make seeds by combining the female ovule with the male sperm, a process called fertilisation. A few plants can make their own seeds, but in most species, the sperm and the ovule have to come from different plants. The plants need help to carry pollen from one plant to another, a process called pollination. Many plants use flying insects to pollinate their flowers. Others use the wind or water.

Bluebells flower each spring, carpeting forest floors with blue. They are pollinated by insects such as bees.

Project Pressing flowers

An artist has used a pressed flower as part of her picture.

A great way to keep a record of flowers is to press them in a book. Lay out the freshly picked flower on a page in the book. Carefully close the book on the flower, making sure that it stays flat to the page. Weigh down the book with some other books and leave it for a couple of weeks. When you return, the flower will have flattened and dried out, and the pressed flower will keep for a long time. You can press more than one flower in the same book, but leave at least 20 pages between each flower. Only ever pick garden flowers. Flowers perform a vital job, and rare ones must be left where they are.

*Animal pollination

Plants that use animals for pollination tempt the animal in with their colours and smell, and give it a reward of sweet nectar for its trouble.

Insect pollinators

The most important pollinators for flowers are insects. Often a plant will use just one kind of insect to pollinate its flowers. The cacao tree for instance, is pollinated by a small fly called a midge. Cacao beans are used to make chocolate, so without midges there would be no chocolate! The most important pollinator of all is the bee. Bees pollinate many different kinds of plant, including much of the food that we eat. Every year, half the honey bees in the whole of the USA are taken to California to pollinate the almond trees there.

As a bee collects sweet nectar from a flower, pollen from the stamen brushes off onto its legs. Pollen from other flowers already on its legs brushes off onto the stigma.

Bird and bat pollinators

Birds and bats are also attracted to flowers by the promise of nectar. A group of birds called hummingbirds are specially adapted to feed only on nectar. They are expert fliers and can hover in the air at just the right angle to collect the nectar with their long beaks. As the birds feed, the plant leaves its pollen on their beaks. Plants that use bats as pollinators produce drab flowers. Bats come out at night, so they cannot see bright colours. The flowers attract the bats by making sweet smells.

A hummingbird hovers in front of a flower to feed.

The biggest flower in the world is a stinky carrion flower produced by the plant titan arum. The flower can grow several metres tall.

Carrion flowers

We give flowers to each other because they look beautiful and often smell beautiful, too. But you would not want to receive a carrion flower as a gift. Carrion flowers smell of rotting flesh. They smell revolting to us, but smell just right to flies and beetles that feed on dead animals. These insects are attracted to the carrion flowers by the stink, and the plant uses them as its pollinators.

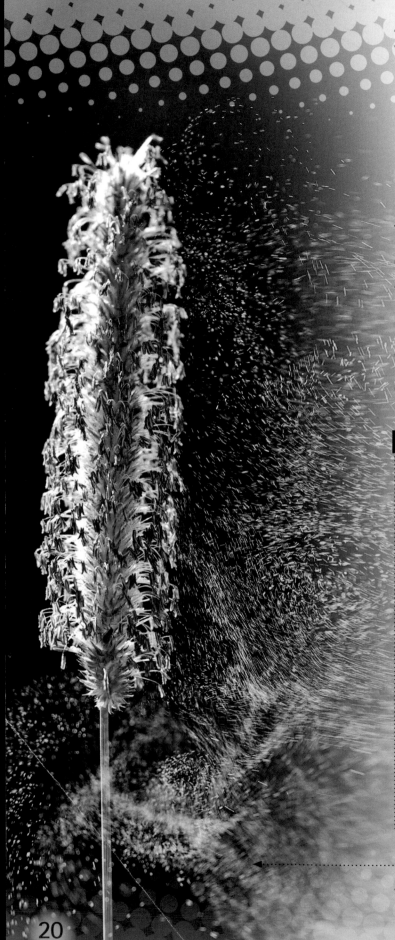

*Wind and water dispersers

Plants that produce drab flowers, such as grasses, do not use animals to spread their pollen. Instead, they use the power of the wind or water to disperse, or carry away, the pollen.

Wind dispersers

Wind pollinators such as grasses produce separate male and female flowers. The pollen is blown away from the exposed stamens of the male flowers. The exposed stigmas of the female flowers are feather-shaped, and catch pollen from the air to fertilise the ovule inside. Wind pollinators waste a lot of pollen, which is often blown high into the atmosphere. They save energy, however, by not growing colourful or scented flowers, and by not making nectar for pollinators to eat.

A grass flower releases its pollen into the wind.

❚ Water dispersers

Most plants that live in the water use animals or wind for pollination. But a few, such as pondweed, release their pollen onto the surface of the water. The pollen is then carried away by the flow of the water, particularly down streams and rivers. Plants that grow entirely beneath the surface of the water, such as waterweed, release their pollen into the water from below the surface.

Waterweed grows just beneath the surface of the water in streams and rivers. It releases its pollen directly into the water.

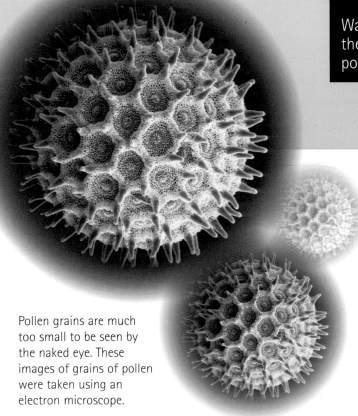

Pollen grains are much too small to be seen by the naked eye. These images of grains of pollen were taken using an electron microscope.

Hayfever

Every spring, many of us start to sneeze and get very itchy eyes. We are suffering from hayfever, which is caused by the tiny grains of pollen that are released into the air by wind dispersers. Our bodies react to the pollen as if it were a dangerous invader that might make us ill. It is this reaction, called an allergic reaction, that causes the itching and sneezing.

*Seeds

Once a flower has been pollinated, it produces seeds. Each seed contains the embryo that will grow into the new plant, and a store of food to give the embryo the energy it needs when it starts growing.

Embryo and food

The flower of a plant has done its job once the ovule has been fertilised. The flower dies and the ovules develop into seeds, which contain a tiny embryo surrounded by some food to help it grow. The embryo and its food (called the endosperm) are protected by a hard seed coat. The food store inside seeds is also an important source of food for animals. Cereal crops, such as wheat, rice and barley, are the seeds of grasses that have been specially bred to produce large, edible seeds.

Cross-section of a hot pepper seed

seed coat

embryo

endosperm

Dispersing the seeds

Once it has made its seeds, the plant needs to find a way to send the seeds away from it. If the seeds just dropped right by the plant, they would not have room or light to grow. Some plants make fruit to disperse their seeds (see page 24). The fruit is eaten by animals and the seed passes through their bodies to be deposited some distance away. Other plants use the wind to carry their seeds away.

The flower of the dandelion has died, leaving behind seeds that have 'parachutes' to help the wind carry them away.

Project Helicopter seeds

The 'blades' need to be folded at an angle so that they face in opposite directions.

The sycamore tree uses the wind to disperse its seeds. The seeds have wings shaped like the blades of a helicopter to carry them away from the tree. You can make your own helicopter seed. You will need a strip of paper, scissors and a paperclip. Fold the paper in half the long way. Cut down the fold to a little less than halfway. Fold each side of the cut paper at opposite angles, as shown left, to make the angled blades of the helicopter. Attach the paperclip to the bottom of the uncut paper to complete your seed. As your seed falls, the air catches the wings, making it spin. Try dropping it from a balcony and see how far away from you it lands.

*Fruit and nuts

Many plants make sweet fruit to distribute their seeds. The fruit is eaten by animals. The seeds contained in the fruit then pass through the animal and end up in the ground with their droppings.

Juicy fruits

The fruit develops from the ovary, part of the carpel, which contains one or more fertilised ovules. The walls of the ovary ripen and often develop into fleshy, sweet-tasting fruit with one or more seeds in it. The fruit is eaten while still on the plant, or falls to the ground to be eaten there. Humans have grown plants for their fruit for thousands of years. By selectively breeding the biggest fruit, we have developed plants that make much larger fruit than in the wild.

We grow many different kinds of fruit in orchards and groves. Oranges are grown in warm places such as Spain or Florida, USA.

Nuts

Nuts are a special kind of fruit in which the ovary wall has developed into a hard shell. Inside the hard shell sits one, or sometimes two, seeds. If animals eat the seeds inside the nut, the seeds are destroyed. As nuts last a long time inside their protective shell, many animals such as squirrels bury them to eat later. The animals will not return to all the nuts they bury, however, and those they do not return to can grow into a new plant.

Nuts such as hazelnuts have a large food store to help the embryo inside grow. This also makes the nut a very rich source of food for animals.

Coconuts

Some trees make very big nuts indeed. Coconut palms produce coconuts, which can grow to the size of a football. Coconuts have a space inside them filled with air. This makes the coconut light enough to float on water. Coconut palms grow near the shore of tropical seas and some of their coconuts fall into the water. They may float in the oceans for thousands of kilometres before they wash ashore. Coconuts have been found washed up as far north as Norway, but it is too cold there for them to grow!

There are more than 2,000 different species of palm tree, including the coconut palm. Coconuts are used in cooking.

*Germination

A seed may lie inactive for months or even years. When conditions are right, it starts to grow. This is known as germination.

The start of a new life

A seed will germinate only if the conditions give it a chance of survival. It may need to be in the soil, but not so deep that there is no oxygen, which it needs to convert its food reserves into energy. It also needs water to break down its food. Each different type of seed needs a particular temperature to germinate, and many also need light. Some seeds will germinate only after there has been a forest fire.

A germinated seed grows into a tiny plant called a seedling. Roots grow downwards, while a stem pushes up.

Barley malt is fermented to make beer.

Barley malt

Beer is made using the germinated seeds of a cereal called barley. The food store inside barley seeds is in the form of a substance called starch. Before the seed can use the starch as energy, it needs to convert it into sugars. Brewers allow the seeds to germinate, then stop the process after a few days. By then the seeds have turned the starch into sugar, but have not yet started using the sugar to grow. The barley is now called malt. Brewers change the sugars in the malt into alcohol by adding yeast in a process called fermentation.

Project Sowing seeds

A sunflower's 'head' actually contains hundreds of tiny flowers, each of which matures to form a seed.

Collect seeds from a flower such as a sunflower that has gone to seed (left). Plant the seeds in different places around your garden at home or at school. Choose light and dark places, damp and dry areas, and try burying the seeds at different depths. Make a note of where you have planted the seeds to see which ones grow. What conditions did the seeds need to germinate? You will have to be patient – depending on the plant you choose, its seeds may not start growing until after winter.

*How we use flowering plants

We grow all kinds of flowering plants for their flowers, seeds or fruit. Many of the plants we grow have been greatly changed over time by selective breeding.

I Food crops

The most important human foods of all are the domesticated grasses, the cereals, such as rice and wheat. Cereals form the main part of the diet of most people around the world. Domesticated cereals have been specially bred to produce large seeds with plenty of food stored in them. Many varieties of domesticated fruit have also been developed, often much larger than their wild cousins. The strawberries we buy in shops may be as large as a table tennis ball. In the wild, strawberries are the size of a pea.

In this paddy field in Kedah, Malaysia, the ground is flooded to grow the cereal crop rice.

The quest for a blue rose

Roses have been bred by humans for 5,000 years, and more than 20,000 different varieties have been developed, most of them red, pink, yellow or white. Over the years, many breeders have tried to create a blue rose by hybridisation, or the breeding together of two different types of rose. They all failed. Then, in 2008, after 20 years of patient research, a team of Japanese scientists grew a blue rose using genetic modification. They took the gene that makes pansies blue and implanted it into a rose.

Flower breeders often have to pollinate their flowers carefully by hand. Here, the breeder is pollinating a rare vanilla orchid.

▌Breeding new plants

Breeders develop new kinds of flowering plant using a process called hybridisation. To make a new hybrid plant, the breeder transfers the pollen of one plant onto the stigma of another one. Recently, scientists have developed a way of making new breeds by altering the plant's genes, the code contained in each of the plant's cells. This is called genetic modification.

The seeds of the wheat plant have been bred to be many times larger than the seeds of wild grass.

*Glossary

Carbohydrates
Substances such as sugars and starch, which give plants the energy to grow.

Digestive juices
Liquid in meat-eating plants that breaks down the bodies of animals.

Domesticated plants
Plants specially bred by humans.

Electron microscope
A powerful microscope that enlarges an image up to 2 million times.

Embryo
The part of a seed that will grow into a new plant.

Fruits
Structures made by a plant to help distribute its seeds. Fruits are often sweet so that animals will eat them.

Germination
The moment a seed starts to develop into a new plant.

Hybrid
A new type of plant developed by crossing two different types of plant.

Nectar
A sweet liquid made inside some flowers to attract animals to them.

Nutrient
A substance such as minerals that a plant needs to stay alive.

Ovary
The base of the carpel in a flower, containing the female ovules.

Petiole
The stalk of a leaf that attaches the blade to the plant's stem.

Photosynthesis
The process by which plants capture the energy of the Sun in their leaves to make the nutrients they need.

Pollen
Tiny grain containing the male sperm.

Spore
A single cell produced by some kinds of simple plants to reproduce.

Tuber
A thickened part of the stem or root that stores food.

*Resources

1000 Things You Should Know About Plants, by John Farndon (Mason Crest, 2002)
A compendium of facts and figures about plants.

Plant, by David Burnie (DK, 2004)
An illustrated guide to plants, part of the Eyewitness series.

The Private Life of Plants, by David Attenborough (BBC, 1995)
A companion to the major BBC TV series of the same name, which looks at how plants grow and move.

Starting Gardening, by Sue Johnson and Cherly Evans (Usborne, 2003)
A guide for young gardeners.

Understanding Plants: Plants and Animals, Plants and Humans, Plants of the World, The Life of Plants, all by Claire Llewellyn (Franklyn Watts, 2009)
A series that explores the important roles plants play in our world.

Earthcycles: Plants, by Sally Morgan (Franklin Watts, 2003)
An exploration of the lifecycles of plants.

Websites

www.bbc.co.uk/schools/ks2bitesize
Games, quizzes and fun revision notes on a wide range of science topics, including flowering plants.

www.bigpicturescience.biz
Learning and teaching ideas on flowering plants and other science topics.

www.scienceprojectideas.co.uk
Ideas for simple projects you can do at home.

www.sciencewithme.com
Games and lots of science project ideas, with worksheets and colouring books to print out.

www.plantsandus.org.uk
Features on lots of different types of plant and the vital role they play in life on Earth.

www.gardeningwithchildren.co.uk
Everything you need to know about starting and maintaining a garden.

Please note: every effort has been made by the publishers to ensure that these websites contain no inappropriate or offensive material. However, because of the nature of the Internet, it is impossible to guarantee that the contents of these sites will not be altered. We strongly advise that Internet access is supervised by a responsible adult.

Index

animals 8, 18–19, 23, 24
aquatic plants 7, 21

barley malt 27
bats 19
beer 27
bees 16, 18
birds 19
blossom 8
bulbs 12

cacao tree 18
carbon dioxide 15
carnivorous plants 11
carpel 16
carrion flowers 19
cells 7
cereal crops 22, 28, 29
chlorophyll 14, 15
coconuts 25

dandelion 23
deciduous trees 9

early plants 5
embryo 22
energy 14, 26

ferns 5
fertilisation 17
flowers 6, 16–17
food 11, 12, 22, 28

fruit 4, 6, 23, 24, 28

genetic modification 29
germination 26–27
grasses 5, 7, 20, 22, 28
gymnosperms 8

hayfever 21
helicopter seeds 23
hummingbirds 19
hybridisation 29

insects 16, 17, 18, 19

leaves 6, 7, 9, 14–15

nectar 18, 19
nutrients 6, 10, 11, 12
nuts 25

ovary 16, 24, 25
ovules 4, 16, 17, 20, 22
oxygen 15, 26

petals 16
petioles 12
phloem 13
photosynthesis 14
plant parts 6–7
pollen 4, 5, 16, 17, 21
pollination 5, 17, 18–21
potatoes 12

pressing flowers 17

root vegetables 11
roots 6, 7, 10–11
roses 29

sap 13
seed 4, 5, 8, 17, 22–26
seed dispersal 23
selective breeding 29
sepals 16
sowing seeds 27
sperm 4, 17
spores 5
stamen 16, 18, 20
starch 11, 27
stems 6, 12–13
stigma 16, 18, 20
sugar 6, 11, 13, 14, 27
sunlight 6, 8, 14, 15
sycamore tree 23

tree rings 9
trees 8–9, 13
tubers 12

water 6, 9, 10, 13, 26
water dispersers 21
wind 5, 17, 21, 23
woody plants 8

xylem 13